THE ADVENTURES OF FERG
Fergie
Frog Scout

by Nancy Cocks • Illustrations by Michael Léveillé

The Frog Scouts were having a contest to see which frog could do the most good deeds in a month. The prize was two tickets to the Flying Squirrel Circus.

Fergie the Frog wanted very much to win, so he tried to be as helpful as he could. He helped Mother Frog clean up the edge of the swamp.

He helped his father clean the flies they caught for supper. He went to visit Grandma Frog and helped her eat mosquito muffins!

Why, Fergie was so helpful, he even did something nice for his big brother, Freddie. He saved three spider leg cookies until Freddie got home from diving practice.

Every time Fergie did something kind or helpful, the frog he helped would check his chart. Even Freddie checked Fergie's chart!

Sure enough, when the month was over, Fergie had done the most good deeds of all the Frog Scouts.

When he gave Fergie the prize, Scout Leader Leather Lips said, "Well done, Ferguson! You really lived up to the Frog Scout promise. Enjoy the Flying Squirrel Circus—and keep up the good work!"

The very next day, Fergie's mother asked him to take some mosquito muffins and juniper jam to his Grandma.

"I'm too tired," said Fergie. "Send Freddie instead." So off went Freddie.

A little while later, Father Frog came in with some water bugs to clean for supper. "Come and help me, Fergie. Then supper will be ready sooner."

"No thanks, Dad," said Fergie. "I'm busy sewing my good deed badge on my Frog Scout hat. I won the prize, you know!"

Finally Mother Frog reminded Fergie it was time to set the round rock table.

"Can't you do it?" Fergie asked. "I've done it every night for the last month. I hate setting the table."

After supper when Fergie said he was tired of drying the dishes too, Father Frog called him over.

"What's this?" he asked. "For a whole month, you were the most helpful little frog in the world. But now you won't lift a web of your foot for anybody else."

"But Dad!" Fergie explained, "The contest is over. I already won the prize. I don't have to be good any more."

"Hmmm," said his father thoughtfully, "when I was a Frog Scout, I learned the promise. Do you remember it, Fergie?"

"Oh sure. I have a badge for saying the promise! 'To be a good and loyal Frog Scout, help other frogs day in and day out'."

"Right," said his father. "Day in and day out. You don't get days off when you're a Frog Scout. Just because the contest is over doesn't mean you can stop helping others. Now go help Freddie dry those dishes."

"Yes, sir," grumbled Fergie.

***

The world would be a pretty unhappy place if we only helped each other on Wednesdays.

Imagine what it would be like if people were only kind to us in February. Imagine how it would feel if we only said 'I love you' on Valentine's Day!

Remember that God's love is for every day. God's love helps us love each other day in and day out!

Dear God, whenever we don't feel like helping, whenever we're tired of being kind, remind us of your love for us. Teach us how to show love for each other each day and every day for Jesus' sake. Amen.